Fondue at Home

The Ultimate Fondue Recipe Book for Amateur Cooks!

BY: Valeria Ray

License Notes

Copyright © 2020 Valeria Ray All Rights Reserved

All rights to the content of this book are reserved by the Author without exception unless permission is given stating otherwise.

The Author have no claims as to the authenticity of the content and the Reader bears all responsibility and risk when following the content. The Author is not liable for any reparations, damages, accidents, injuries or other incidents occurring from the Reader following all or part of this publication.

Table of Contents

Introduction 6

    Classic Cheese Fondue 7

    Swiss cheese Fondue 9

    Sausage Fondue Breakfast 11

    Gouda and Mushroom Fondue 13

    Queso Fundido 15

    Smoked Mozzarella Fondue 18

    Breakfast Fun-Due 20

    Porcini Fondue 22

    Mini-Waffle Fondue 25

    Oka Cheese Fondue 27

    Cinnamon Roll Breakfast Fondue 29

    Cheeseburger Fondue 31

    Tomato & Olive Oil Fondue 33

    White Wine & Blue Cheese Fondue 35

Chicken & Beef Fondue 37

Fireball Fondue 40

Roast Pumpkin with Cheese "Fondue" 42

Spinach and Artichoke Fondue 45

Pizza Fondue 47

Buffalo Cheese Fondue 49

Neuchâtel Two Cheese Fondue 51

Dark Chocolate Fondue 53

Nutella Chocolate Fondue 55

Caramel Fondue 57

Pineapple Upside-Down 59

La Dolce Vita 61

Philly's Phave 63

Chorizo Fondue 65

Copycat Olive Garden Fondue 67

Dijon Lamb Fondue 69

Conclusion 71

About the Author 72

Author's Afterthoughts 73

Introduction

How can you integrate fondue dishes into your recipe repertoire at home? Do you want to work with the different and new ingredients? Do you curious about the various ways in which using a fondue pot can make your recipes more interesting?

If you love creamy, rich chocolate, and cheeses, grab some family members or friends and have a fondue party, or just a fondue dinner. You can share cocktails, conversation, and some VERY tasty food.

Read on and discover delicious recipes to try out on your fondue pot!

Classic Cheese Fondue

A classic recipe for starters! This delicious cheese fondue combines a few yummy cheeses to bring you a melty pot of deliciousness!

Serves: 12

Time: 30m

Ingredients:

- 3 cups Alpine-style cheese, grated
- 3 cups gouda cheese, grated
- 3 cups fontina cheese, grated
- 4 tbsp. corn starch
- 2 cloves garlic, peeled, minced
- 2 tbsp. brandy
- ¼ tsp ground nutmeg
- 2 cups dry white wine
- 2 tbsp. freshly squeezed lemon juice
- 2 teaspoons Dijon mustard

Directions:

Add all the varieties of cheese into a bowl. Sprinkle corn starch over the cheese and toss well.

Place a heatproof fondue pot or heavy saucepan over medium-low heat. Add wine, lemon juice and garlic and stir.

When the mixture begins to simmer, add the cheese mixture into the pot, a tablespoon at a time and mix well each time.

When all of it is added, stir until smooth.

Add brandy, nutmeg and mustard and stir well.

Turn off the heat. Serve warm.

Swiss cheese Fondue

Swiss cheese? Yes, please!

Serves: 4

Time: 30m

Ingredients:

- 1 small clove garlic, peeled, halved
- 3 teaspoons corn starch
- 1/8 tsp ground nutmeg
- ½ cup dry white wine
- ½ tsp freshly squeezed lemon juice
- Freshly ground pepper to taste
- ¾ tablespoon kirsch
- 1 cup Emmental cheese or any other Swiss cheese, grated
- 2 ½ cups gruyere cheese, grated

Directions:

Cut garlic into 2 halves and rub the inside of the fondue pot with it. Throw away the garlic cloves.

Add all the varieties of cheese into the fondue pot. Add lemon juice, corn starch and wine and whisk well.

Place the pot over medium-low heat. Cook until cheese begins to melt. Stir occasionally.

Stir in kirsch, nutmeg and pepper and stir until smooth. Turn off the heat.

Serve hot.

Sausage Fondue Breakfast

This breakfast is handy since you can make most of it the night before. It's also great for special occasions and holidays.

Makes 4-5 Servings (It Makes many cubes)

Time: 9 hours and 15 minutes including 8 hours of refrigeration time

Ingredients:

- 1/2 cup of milk, whole
- 1 x 10.5-oz. can of cream o' mushroom soup
- 3/4 tsp. of mustard
- 2 & 1/4 cups of milk, whole
- 5 large eggs
- 2 pounds of sausage links, cut in thirds and browned & drained
- 2 cups of grated sharp or medium cheese
- 9 cubed slices of sourdough bread

Instructions:

Spray or grease sides and bottom of 13x9 baking dish.

Arrange the bread in bottom of dish. Top with the sausage and cheese.

Beat the eggs. Add mustard and milk. Pour the mixture over the sausage, bread and cheese. Refrigerate the dish overnight.

When you are ready to make, dilute the mushroom soup with some milk. Pour over the rest of the mixture. Bake for an hour or until it sets in 350F oven. Serve with deep dish and sticks/forks.

Gouda and Mushroom Fondue

Forget the idea that all fondues are "just cheese." This one is different. The mushrooms and white wine add a special taste that you won't find with plain cheese, and you'll want to buy some extra bread to dip.

Makes: 4 Servings

Time: 25 minutes

Ingredients:

- 1 & 1/3 cups of cheese, Gouda, diced
- 3 tbsp. of cream, heavy
- 1 cup of trimmed, cleaned mushrooms
- 1 tbsp. of oil, olive
- 2 tbsp. of wine, white
- Bread for serving
- Salt & pepper, as desired

Instructions:

Preheat oven to 375F.

In oven-safe, medium skillet heat olive oil on med. heat.

Add mushrooms. Season using salt & pepper. Sauté until almost tender, or about four to five minutes.

Deglaze pan using white wine. Bring mixture to simmer. Wine should be nearly absorbed. Whisk in heavy cream. Simmer again.

Add Gouda cheese. Place skillet in oven. Bake until cheese melts. Serve with bread for handy dipping.

Queso Fundido

This delicious queso fondue is the best of both worlds!

Serves: 12 – 15

Time: 40m

Ingredients:

- 2 small tomatoes, chopped
- 4 tbsp. chopped fresh oregano
- 4 ½ cups Monterey cheese, grated
- 4 ½ cups mild yellow cheddar, grated
- 2 sausage links (114 grams each), discard casing
- 1 cup lager beer
- 2 Serrano chilies, deseeded, chopped
- Kosher salt to taste
- 2 tbsp. all-purpose flour
- 1 cup minced onions

Directions:

For salsa: Add tomatoes, oregano, salt and chili into a bowl and mix well. Cover and set aside for a while for the flavours to blend in.

Place both the types of cheese in a bowl. Sprinkle flour over it. Toss well.

Place a saucepan over medium heat. Add in the chorizo. Continue cooking for a couple of minutes. Break it simultaneously as it cooks.

Stir in the onions and cook until pink. Remove using a slotted spoon.

Pour beer into the saucepan. Scrape the bottom of the saucepan to remove any browned bits that may be stuck to it.

Add the cheese mixture into the pot, 3 – 4 tbsp. at a time and mix well each time.

When all of it is added, stir until smooth.

Add chorizo back into the saucepan. Mix well. Turn off the heat.

Let it rest for a few minutes.

Spread salsa over the queso fundido and serve.

Smoked Mozzarella Fondue

This cheese fondue combines 3 delicious cheeses to bring you the perfect creamy stretchy fondue!

Serves: 3 – 4

Time: 20m

Ingredients:

- 1 1/4 cup cream cheese, at room temperature
- ½ cup grated provolone cheese
- ½ cup smoked mozzarella cheese
- ¼ cup freshly grated parmesan cheese
- ¼ tsp dried thyme
- 1/8 tsp red pepper flakes
- Freshly ground pepper to taste
- ¼ tsp Italian seasoning
- Salt to taste
- ½ tbsp. finely chopped parsley
- 3 tbsp. sour cream
- ½ small tomato, chopped

Directions:

Add cream cheese, sour cream, seasonings, salt, thyme and all the cheeses into a baking dish and mix until well combined.

Bake in a preheated oven at for 20 minutes, at 350° F

Set the oven to broil mode and broil for a few minutes until brown on top.

Top with tomato and parsley and serve.

Breakfast Fun-Due

What a great way to celebrate the summer! Let your kids help prepare doughnut holes and their favorite fruits on sticks, and then dip them in an easy-to-make chocolate sauce.

Makes: 4 Servings

Time: 10 minutes

Ingredients:

- Assorted fruits, like strawberries, melon, grapes and bananas
- Mini doughnuts or doughnut holes

For fondue skewers:

- Wooden skewers or lollipop sticks

For the chocolate fondue:

- 5 tbsp. of honey, organic
- 1/2 cup of whipping cream, heavy
- 2 cups of chocolate chips, semi-sweet

Instructions:

Skewer the doughnut holes and fruit. Set them aside.

In micro-wave safe large bowl, combine cream and chocolate chips. Microwave it for three or four minutes. Stop every 1/2-minute to stir. Keep the mixture smooth.

Add in the honey. Sauce is too thick? Add in a little more or add some milk.

Divide the mixture into four small bowls. Serve with sticks and dipping ingredients.

Porcini Fondue

Mushrooms and cheese are an old combination and we can see why – they're delicious!

Serves: 3

Time: 20m

Ingredients:

- ¼ cup dried porcini mushrooms
- ½ cup hot water
- 2 small cloves garlic, peeled, minced
- 1 tsp corn starch
- 1 cup grated, packed Emmental cheese
- 1 cup grated, packed Gruyere cheese
- 10 tbsp. Sauvignon Blank or any other dry white wine of your choice
- Salt to taste
- Pepper to taste

Directions:

Place porcini mushrooms in a bowl. Pour hot water over it. Let it rehydrate for about 30 minutes.

Take out the mushrooms from the soaked water and place on your cutting board. Chop into fine pieces. Do not discard the soaked water.

Pour the soaked water into a skillet, but do not add the particles that are at the bottom of the bowl.

Add mushrooms into the skillet along with garlic. Place the skillet over medium heat and cook until nearly dry. Add salt and pepper to taste. Turn off the heat.

Meanwhile, add all the cheeses into a bowl and toss well.

Add ½ tablespoon wine and corn starch into a bowl and stir well.

Pour remaining wine into a saucepan. Place the saucepan over medium-high heat.

Add the cheese mixture into the pot, 3 – 4 tbsp. at a time and mix well each time.

When all of it is added, stir until smooth. Stir in the corn starch mixture.

Stir constantly until slightly thick. Simmer for a couple of minutes. Taste and adjust the seasonings if required. Turn off the heat.

Transfer into a serving bowl. Add porcini and stir.

Serve hot or warm. It tastes great with ham and Ciabatta.

Mini-Waffle Fondue

This breakfast-time fondue will wake up your sleepy mind. It's nourishing and easy since the fruit sauce takes only minutes to prepare. You'll be surprised at how much young children enjoy this breakfast, too. They love (supervised) dipping.

Makes: 4 Servings

Time: 30 minutes

Ingredients:

- 12 mini-waffles, mini-pancakes or fingers of French toast
- 1 pinch ground cinnamon
- 1/4 tsp. of vanilla extract, pure
- 2 tbsp. of cream cheese, light, whipped
- 1/3 cup of syrup, maple or your favorite
- 1 x 15-oz. can of peaches, sliced – use juice, too

Instructions:

Combine the cinnamon, vanilla, cream cheese, syrup and peaches in food processor. Purée until the mixture is smooth. There can be some cheese lumps showing at this time. They'll be gone in step 2.

Pour mixture into pot. Warm on med-high and stir often until cream cheese has melted and sauce bubbles around edges.

Serve in large bowl with mini-waffles or mini pancakes.

Use fingers for dipping, but don't double-dip.

Oka Cheese Fondue

The Oka cheese in this fondue pairs perfectly with the wine!

Serves: 4 – 5

Time: 20m

Ingredients:

- ½ cup + 2 tbsp. heavy cream
- ¼ cup iced wine, Canadian if possible
- ¼ cup dry white wine
- 1 ½ cup Oka cheese or Port-Salut cheese, remove rind, coarsely grate the cheese
- 1 ½ tbsp. all-purpose flour

Directions:

Add cream, flour and both the wines into a heavy saucepan. Place the saucepan over medium heat.

Stir constantly and cook until thick.

Stir in the cheese, 2 – 3 heaping tbsp. at a time and cook until cheese melts each time. Whisk well until smooth.

Transfer into a fondue pot and serve.

Cinnamon Roll Breakfast Fondue

This is a simple fondue recipe for breakfast time. It's a great way to feed the troops over the weekend or during the week if time allows.

Makes: 4 Servings

Time: 35 minutes

Ingredients:

- 1 x 6-oz. carton of yogurt, honey vanilla, Greek
- 1/2 cup of crushed cereal of choice
- 1 cup of strawberries
- 2 sliced bananas
- 1 sliced green apple
- 1 tube of cinnamon rolls and icing

Instructions:

Preheat the oven to 400F.

Cover medium baking sheet using parchment paper.

Open cinnamon rolls. Slice all rounds into four pieces. Bake in oven for 10 to 14 minutes. They should be just starting to turn brown.

Set your table with small bowls of fruit, cinnamon roll cubes, cereal and yogurt.

Serve with fondue skewers. Mixing and dipping is a fun breakfast, especially on the weekend, when you won't have to hurry.

Cheeseburger Fondue

Take frozen meatballs and transform them into cheeseburger with this cheesy fondue. You can serve them with toothpicks or fondue forks. The meatballs can be dipped in diced tomatoes, pickle relish, and cheese.

Makes: 4 Servings

Time: 25 minutes

Ingredients:

- 1/4 cup of diced tomatoes, fire roasted
- 1/4 cup of lettuce, shredded
- 1/4 cup of relish, pickle
- 30 frozen meatballs – cook using directions on the package
- 1 cup of cheddar cheese, grated
- 3/4 cup of beer, light
- 1/4 tsp. of Worcestershire sauce
- 2 tbsp. of flour, all-purpose
- 1/4 tsp. of mustard, ground
- 2 tbsp. of butter, softened

Instructions:

Add butter to saucepan on medium heat. Allow to melt. Whisk in flour. Cook for a minute.

Add beer, Worcestershire sauce and mustard. Whisk continuously until the mixture thickens, in two minutes or so.

Remove from the burner. Stir in cheddar cheese. Continue to stir until the sauce is creamy and smooth. Place in fondue pot or slow cooker to keep it warm.

Serve meatballs with toothpicks or fondue forks. Dip meatballs in cheese, then diced tomatoes, lettuce and pickle relish.

Tomato & Olive Oil Fondue

Tomato fondue is even easier than cheese fondue. It's also versatile and tasty. The communal fondue pot offers an excellent way to enjoy this classic veggie mix. The cherry tomatoes should be cooked slowly in butter.

Makes: 6 Servings

Time: 15 minutes

Ingredients:

- 4 tbsp. of oil, olive
- 2 pints of tomatoes, cherry
- 1/2 tsp. of salt, kosher
- 1/4 cup of butter, unsalted
- Crusty bread, sliced

Instructions:

Combine the oil and tomatoes in skillet on high heat. Stir often while cooking until the tomatoes have begun to burst, which usually takes about five or six minutes.

Reduce the heat to med-high. Cook and stir often until most tomatoes have broken down, or five to seven minutes.

Stir in the salt and butter until butter melts.

Remove from oven burner. Pour mixture into fondue pot. Serve while hot, with crusty bread.

White Wine & Blue Cheese Fondue

Making enjoyable fondue dishes will earn you the admiration of your recipe-loving friends and family members. Not as many people fondue as they did back in the day, but the bubbling pot of simmering cheese and white wine will make any evening a party. Dip responsibly.

Makes: 12 Servings

Time: 20 minutes

Ingredients:

- 2 tbsp. of crème fraiche
- 2 tbsp. + 2 tsp. of corn starch
- 12 oz. of crumbled cheese, British Stilton
- 1 cup of Sauternes
- 1 garlic clove
- Sea salt & pepper, ground

For serving: cubed bread, pickled veggies, beef tips and fingerling potatoes

Instructions:

Rub inside of fondue pot vigorously with garlic. Discard garlic. Add Sauternes. Bring to boil on med. heat.

In small bowl, stir corn starch and Stilton cheese and combine. Once Sauternes comes to boil, add cheese mixture slowly, whisking well. Make sure that every addition has been melted and combined before you add more.

Once you have added all cheese, cook for another minute. Whisk in the crème fraiche, then season using salt & pepper.

Remove heat from pot. Serve with bread and other dippable ingredients of choice.

Chicken & Beef Fondue

Chicken & beef fondue is a delicious, quick dinner that is like a classic cheesy fondue remade for carnivores. The variety of flavors in the sauce makes it a bit sweet and somewhat tangy at the same time. You can slice the meat thinly for this recipe or dice it. Cubed bread works well, too. Don't add too much food at one time, or the meat won't cook properly.

Makes: 8 Servings

Time: 2 hours & 35 minutes

Ingredients:

For cucumber sauce

- 1/2 tsp. of sea salt
- 2 tbsp. of onion, chopped
- 1 cup of cucumber, peeled and chopped
- 1/4 cup of milk, whole
- 2 cups of sour cream
- 2 pkgs. of softened cream cheese

For fondue sauce

- 4 tsp. of parsley flakes
- 4 peeled garlic cloves
- 2 x 14-ounce cans of broth, beef
- 4 x 14-ounce cans of broth, chicken
- 2 cups of broccoli florets, fresh, small
- 2 sliced carrots, medium
- 2 cubed bell peppers, your favorite color
- 1 x 8-ounce pkg. of mushrooms, fresh, whole
- 1 pound of chicken breasts, skinless, boneless
- 1 pound of sirloin steak, beef, boneless
- 2 tsp. of thyme leaves, dried
- 1/3 tsp. of salt, coarse
- 1/3 tsp. of pepper, ground

Other dipping sauces as preferred:

- Teriyaki sauce
- Sweet & sour sauce
- Horseradish sauce
- BBQ sauce

Instructions:

To create the sauce, beat cream cheese 'til creamy in a medium-sized bowl. Stir in the other sauce ingredients. Cover. Refrigerate for two hours or so, until it chills.

Cut the chicken and beef into cubes. Blot them dry using paper towels. Place leaves of lettuce on a platter and arrange meat on them. Cover and refrigerate until you're ready to serve.

Arrange the veggies on another plate. Set it aside.

When ready to serve, divide the broth into two x 3-quart fondue pots. Add roughly 1/2 of salt, pepper, parsley and garlic in each pot. Heat until the mixture is boiling in both pots.

Use fondue forks to spear veggies and meats and dip in hot broth. Cook them for two to four minutes until the meat cooks. Serve with dipping sauces.

Fireball Fondue

This one is not for the kids, people… The Fireball whiskey really gives it a kick. Use the best quality ingredients to gain the most enjoyment. You can even use holiday loaf (fruitcake) in cubes, on skewers or sticks, to help you enjoy the fiery fondue.

Serves: 6

Time: 40m

Ingredients:

- ¾ cup grated white cheddar cheese
- ¾ cup grated cheddar cheese
- 1 tablespoon Fireball whiskey
- ½ cup lager beer
- 1 tablespoon corn starch
- ½ tablespoon hot sauce

Directions:

Add all the varieties of cheese into a bowl. Sprinkle corn starch over the cheese and toss well.

Place a heatproof fondue pot or heavy saucepan over medium-low heat. Add beer and let it heat.

When the mixture begins to simmer, add the cheese mixture into the pot, 2 – 3 heaping tablespoons at a time and mix well each time.

When all of it is added, stir until smooth.

Turn off the heat.

Roast Pumpkin with Cheese "Fondue"

This fondue is an absolute favorite for everyone!

Serves: 16

Time: 1hr

Ingredients:

- 2 baguettes (15 inches each), cut into ½ inch thick slices
- 3 cups heavy cream
- 1 teaspoon grated nutmeg
- 5 cups coarsely grated Emmentaler cheese
- 5 cups coarsely grated Gruyere cheese
- 2 tablespoons olive oil
- 2 orange pumpkins (3.2 kilograms each)
- 2 cups chicken or vegetable broth
- Salt to taste
- Pepper to taste

Directions:

Place the baguette slices on a baking sheet, in a single layer.

Bake in a preheated oven at 450° F for 7 minutes or until crisp on top.

Remove from the oven and let aside to cool.

Cut off a thick, round slice, from the stem side of each of the pumpkin. Retain the tops.

Scoop the seeds and membranes from the inside of the pumpkins as well as from the tops of the pumpkins.

Sprinkle salt inside the pumpkin.

Add both the cheeses into a bowl and toss well.

Add broth, cream, nutmeg, pepper and salt into a bowl and whisk well.

Place a layer of bread on the bottom of the pumpkins. Do not overlap.

Sprinkle a cup of cheese over the bread in each of the pumpkins. Spread ½ cup cream mixture over the cheese layer in each pumpkin.

Repeat steps 9 – 10 a few times until the pumpkin is nearly full.

Close the pumpkins with the tops.

Place rack on the lower third position in the oven.

Grease 2 baking pans with some oil. Grease the pumpkin with oil on the skin side.

Bake in a preheated oven at 350° F for about 1 – 2 hours or until the pumpkin is tender.

Scoop some of the pumpkin along with the layered fondue while serving.

Spinach and Artichoke Fondue

This popular fondue recipe uses cheeses that are easy to find in Parmesan, Gruyere, and mozzarella. The dip is completed by the addition of garlic, artichokes, and spinach. It CAN be made with chicken broth, but that sometimes detracts from the stringiness of the cheese that you get when you use white wine.

Serves: 8

Time: 40m

Ingredients:

- 1 cup shredded mozzarella cheese
- 1 cup shredded gruyere cheese
- ½ cup shredded parmesan cheese
- 2/3 cup white cooking wine
- 2 teaspoons flour
- 2 tablespoons minced garlic
- 2/3 cup chopped, drained artichoke hearts
- 1 ½ cups chopped baby spinach

Directions:

Add all the varieties of cheese into a bowl and toss well.

Sprinkle flour on top. Toss well.

Add wine and garlic into a fondue pot or heavy pot. Place the pot over medium-high flame.

When it begins to boil, add spinach and artichoke hearts and mix well.

Cook until spinach wilts. Add the cheese mixture into the pot, 2 – 3 heaping tablespoons at a time and mix well each time.

Stir constantly until the cheese melts and resembles strings.

Serve hot.

Pizza Fondue

What a marriage – pizza and fondue! These are two foods that are both fun to eat, and they bring people together for parties or dinners. If your cheese doesn't melt quickly enough in your fondue pot, transfer it to a pan and heat it on medium heat on the stove. Then, when you pour it back into the fondue pot, and it will help in keeping the pot warm.

Serves: 3 – 4

Time: 20m

Ingredients:

- ½ jar marinara sauce
- 3 tablespoons freshly grated parmesan cheese
- 1 cup shredded mozzarella cheese + extra to top
- ½ package mini pepperoni
- A large pinch dried oregano

Directions:

Add marinara sauce, oregano, both the cheeses and half the pepperoni into the fondue pot or heavy bottomed saucepan.

Place the pot over medium heat. Stir frequently until the mixture melts. Turn off the heat.

Garnish with mozzarella and pepperoni slices and serve.

Buffalo Cheese Fondue

A fantastic option for the game nights! Serve with crispy chicken tenders to really seal the deal.

Serves: 12

Time: 30m

Ingredients:

- 3 cups Alpine-style cheese, grated
- 3 cups gouda cheese, grated
- 3 cups fontina cheese, grated
- 4 tbsp. corn starch
- 4 cups hot sauce

Directions:

Add all the varieties of cheese into a bowl. Sprinkle corn starch over the cheese and toss well.

Place a heatproof fondue pot or heavy saucepan over medium-low heat.

When the mixture begins to simmer, add the cheese mixture into the pot, a tablespoon at a time and mix well each time.

When all of it is added, stir until smooth. Add in the hot sauce. Stir well.

Turn off the heat. Serve warm.

Neuchâtel Two Cheese Fondue

Delicious two cheese Swiss fondue with Gruyère and Emmental cheese.

Makes: 4 servings

Prep: 5 mins

Cook: 10 mins

Ingredients:

- ½ pound Emmental cheese, diced
- 2 tablespoons kirsch
- ½ pound Gruyère cheese, diced
- ¼ teaspoon nutmeg
- 1 garlic clove
- A pinch of black pepper
- 1 cup dry white wine
- 1 large parsley sprig, minced
- 2 teaspoons lemon juice
- Toasted Bread Cubes
- 1½ tablespoons cornstarch

Directions:

Smash the garlic & cut in half.

Rub the garlic around inside of med saucepan. Discard. Add the wine to the pan and cook on low heat. Don't allow the wine to boil.

When warm, add in the lemon juice. Add the cheese. Stir the cheese continually in a sideways figure 8 pattern. Wait until the cheese is completely melted when adding more. Do not allow the fondue mixture to boil.

When melted, dissolve the corn starch in 2 tbsp. kirsch and stir into the cheese. Increase the heat until it is bubbling and starting to thicken. Stir in the nutmeg, black pepper, and parsley. Transfer to the fondue pot and set on the burner. Serve with the bread cubes for dipping.

Dark Chocolate Fondue

This is a mouthwatering, unconventional end to a meal – it's so much more than a simple dessert. It brings people together over sharing food. You can set out plates for your family or a couple guests and enjoy this smaller-than-party size fondue – or make a double recipe and invite some more people in on the fun.

Makes: 8 Servings

Time: 10 minutes

Ingredients:

- 2 cups of cream, heavy
- 1 lb. of dark chocolate

Instructions:

Combine cream and chocolate in heat-proof, medium sized bowl set over pan of gently simmering water.

Use a wooden spoon to stir now and then, until all the chocolate has melted and the mixture becomes smooth.

Divide among eight small ramekins or bowls. Serve with dipping ingredients.

Nutella Chocolate Fondue

This is a total crowd pleaser! Nutella and chocolate? Count us in!

Makes: 8 Servings

Time: 10 minutes

Ingredients:

- 2 cups of cream, heavy
- ½ cup milk chocolate
- 2 cups Nutella

Instructions:

Combine cream and chocolate in heat-proof, medium sized bowl set over pan of gently simmering water.

Use a wooden spoon to stir now and then, until all the chocolate has melted and the mixture becomes smooth.

Stir in the Nutella.

Divide among eight small ramekins or bowls. Serve with dipping ingredients such as fresh strawberries or banana slices!

Caramel Fondue

Who doesn't love a totally different dessert fondue? It will be a favorite as soon as your friends and family taste it for the first time. You often see dessert fondues at events and parties, but this one is simple to make, so you can easily have it at home.

Makes: 8 Servings

Time: 20 minutes

Ingredients:

- 1 tsp. of vanilla extract, pure
- 1/2 tsp. of salt, coarse
- 1/2 cup of sugar, dark brown
- 4 tbsp. of butter, softened
- 2/3 cup of cream

For dipping

- Marshmallows
- Fruit, like berries, bananas, etc.
- Pound cake
- Doughnut holes

Instructions:

Combine all ingredients except vanilla and salt in heavy pot.

Cook on low until sugar dissolves. Don't allow the mixture to boil.

Bring sauce to simmer for three to four minutes.

Remove from heat. Whisk in vanilla extract and salt.

Serve warm with finger foods for dipping.

Pineapple Upside-Down

Nothing beats the combination of caramel, pineapple, and rich buttery cake, especially if there's a little rum thrown in for kicks. Don't skimp on the rum a dark, flavorful Caribbean rum like Gosling's or Appleton Estate will add flavor and dimension, rather than just burning sinuses. When cooking the caramel, keep a plain white plate nearby to check the color. As the caramel cooks, drizzle a little of it onto the plate—it should be deep amber, not golden or brown.

Makes: 3 cups

Time: 20m

Ingredients:

- 1¼ cups heavy cream
- 1½ cups sugar
- ½ cup water
- 2 teaspoons light corn syrup
- 2 to 3 tablespoons dark rum
- 1 teaspoon vanilla extract

Instructions:

In a heavy saucepan, add cream and bring to a boil over med-high heat and remove it from the heat.

In a separate deep, heavy saucepan (one with a light interior so you can see the color of the sugar as it cooks), combine the sugar, water, and corn syrup. Cover and bring to a boil over medium-high heat.

Remove the cover and cook the sugar without stirring until it starts to turn golden around the edges, 5 to 8 minutes. Swirl the pan around to ensure even cooking. When the sugar is deep amber, add the cream—be careful, the mixture will bubble up and steam.

Stir the caramel until it is uniform and all the sugar has dissolved, returning it to heat if needed to melt any lumps.

Move pan from heat and stir in the rum and vanilla. Immediately transfer the caramel to a fondue pot and serve, or cool to room temperature before transferring to a storage container.

The fondue can be made up to 2 days ahead. To serve, reheat in a saucepan over medium-low heat, stirring frequently, until fluid.

Serve warm with fresh pineapple slices and pound cake!

La Dolce Vita

Creamy and extravagant, a triple-crème cheese such as the French Saint-André or Mt. Tam from California's Cowgirl Creamery served with fruit can be a simple, sophisticated dessert. Add a touch of honey, anise seed, and a splash of vin santo, and you've got a fondue fit for a king.

Makes: 3 cups

Time: 30m

Ingredients:

- ½ cup plus 2 tablespoons vin santo
- 2 tablespoons honey
- ¼ teaspoon anise seed
- 1½ pounds Saint-André, Cowgirl Creamery Mt. Tam, or other triple-crème cheese, rind discarded and cubed

Instructions:

In a heavy saucepan, combine the vin santo, honey, and anise seed. Bring to a boil over high heat, then decrease the heat to low.

Add the cheese to the wine mixture, a chunk at a time, whisking constantly to melt the cheese before the next addition.

When all the cheese has been added, whisk until smooth. Transfer immediately to a fondue pot and serve.

Philly's Phave

This departure from tradition should have both cheesesteak and fondue purists up in arms, but they won't be able to resist its cheesy charm. If you want to go a little more traditional, try it with American Cheddar or provolone in place of the stinky European varieties used here.

Makes: about 4 cups

Time: 20m

Ingredients:

- 8 ounces each raclette and Emmental, or 16 ounces Cheddar or provolone, grated
- 6 spring onions, minced
- 2 tablespoons olive oil
- 1 onion, diced
- 1 green bell pepper, diced
- 2 cups coarsely chopped mushrooms
- Kosher salt and freshly ground black pepper
- 2 tablespoons all-purpose flour
- 1½ cups beef stock

Instructions:

Combine all cheeses and set aside. In a fondue pot, heat the oil over medium-high heat. Add the green onions, onion, bell pepper, and mushrooms and cook, stirring, until slightly softened, about 5 to 8 minutes.

Season with salt and pepper to taste. Add in flour. Cook, stirring frequently, until all the moisture is gone from the mushrooms, 4 to 5 minutes.

Add the beef stock and stir until the mixture comes to a boil. Decrease the heat to medium-low and add the cheese mixture, ½ cup at a time, stirring until melted after each addition. Serve immediately.

SERVE WITH: toasted Italian or French bread cubes • cooked beef steak or roast, cut into bite-size cubes (great for leftover prime rib) • assorted pickles • cooked Italian sausages, cut into bite-size pieces

Chorizo Fondue

Red bell pepper, Mexican chorizo, and roasted poblano chilies make this fondue special. It can be served with bell pepper strips and tortilla chips for dipping or choose other favorites.

Makes: 6 Servings

Cooking + Prep Time: 35 minutes

Ingredients:

- Warmed corn tortillas to serve, small
- 1 bell pepper, red
- 3/4 pound of Mexican chorizo, crumbled, casings removed
- 1 chili, poblano
- 2 lbs. of shredded cheese, Monterey Jack

Instructions:

Place bell pepper and chilies over flame of gas burner on a high heat. Roast them, turning, until blackened. Transfer to medium bowl. Cover with cling wrap. Set aside and allow to steam for about 15 minutes. Peel the peppers and discard the stems, ribs, skins and seeds. Cut in 1/4-inch strips and set them aside.

Heat medium saucepan on med-high. Add chorizo. Cook for two or three minutes.

Lower heat. Add pepper strips and cheese. Stir while cooking until the cheese melts.

Dip rolled tortillas into cheese mixture in fondue pot.

Copycat Olive Garden Fondue

This is an unashamed copy of the "Mozzarella Fonduta" recipe served at Olive Garden. It uses sour cream and Italian cheeses to create a cheesy, creamy appetizer that is SO hard to resist. If you've tried it in the restaurant, you'll love the in-home version, too.

Makes: 6-8 Servings

Cooking + Prep Time: 35 minutes

Ingredients:

- 1 chopped tomato, small
- 1/4 tsp. of pepper flakes, red
- 1/2 tsp. of seasoning, Italian
- 1/2 tsp. of thyme, dried
- 1/3 cup of sour cream
- 1/2 cup of Parmesan, grated
- 1 cup of provolone
- 1 cup of mozzarella, smoked
- 8 ounces of softened cream cheese
- 1 tbsp. of chopped parsley
- Salt, kosher
- Black pepper, ground

Instructions:

Preheat the oven to 350F.

Combine cheeses, cream cheese, red pepper flakes, Italian seasoning, sour cream and thyme in large bowl. Stir until combined fully. Season using salt & pepper.

Transfer the cheese mixture into small skillet. Cook 'til cheese bubbles, about 20 to 25 minutes.

Pour into fondue pot. Garnish with parsley and tomato. Serve with a cubed baguette or other dippers.

Dijon Lamb Fondue

This recipe uses classic French marinade and tender lamb to create a meat fondue that you'll enjoy through all the cooler months of the year. Be careful not to overcook your lamb. It will only take one or two minutes in hot oil. Then allow it to cool a bit before enjoying the taste.

Makes: 4 Servings

Cooking + Prep Time: 20 minutes + marinating time

Ingredients:

- 1 lb. of cubed lamb leg or loin
- Oil to fondue

For marinade:

- 1 tbsp. of garlic powder
- 1 tbsp. of onion flakes, dried
- Rosemary, fresh, chopped
- 2 tbsp. of vinegar, white wine
- 1/4 cup of mustard, Dijon
- Sea salt & black pepper, ground, as desired

Instructions:

Combine salt, pepper, garlic powder, onion flakes, rosemary, vinegar and mustard in medium bowl. Mix until combined.

In casserole dish, pour marinade over the lamb, coating it well. Cover. Refrigerate for an hour or more.

Heat oil to 375F in saucepan. Transfer to the fondue pot. Don't fill the fondue pot higher than 1/2 full.

Spear the lamb cubes with the fondue forks for a couple minutes until they are cooked to your desired level of doneness.

Conclusion

We're now at the end of this delicious fondue recipe book! This fondue-centric cookbook has shown you how to use different ingredients to affect sweet or spicy tastes in fondue sauces. Cheese fondues are pretty commonplace, so we hope the additional new flavors will be something you enjoy working with!

Whether you are using meatballs, bread cubes, chocolate, or the many other possible dippers, you'll enjoy new experiences. Test out different accompaniments to your fondues. The possibilities are endless!

About the Author

A native of Indianapolis, Indiana, Valeria Ray found her passion for cooking while she was studying English Literature at Oakland City University. She decided to try a cooking course with her friends and the experience changed her forever. She enrolled at the Art Institute of Indiana which offered extensive courses in the culinary Arts. Once Ray dipped her toe in the cooking world, she never looked back.

When Valeria graduated, she worked in French restaurants in the Indianapolis area until she became the head chef at one of the 5-star establishments in the area. Valeria's attention to taste and visual detail caught the eye of a local business person who expressed an interest in publishing her recipes. Valeria began her secondary career authoring cookbooks and e-books which she tackled with as much talent and gusto as her first career. Her passion for food leaps off the page of her books which have colourful anecdotes and stunning pictures of dishes she has prepared herself.

Valeria Ray lives in Indianapolis with her husband of 15 years, Tom, her daughter, Isobel and their loveable Golden Retriever, Goldy. Valeria enjoys cooking special dishes in her large, comfortable kitchen where the family gets involved in preparing meals. This successful, dynamic chef is an inspiration to culinary students and novice cooks everywhere.

Author's Afterthoughts

Thank you for Purchasing my book and taking the time to read it from front to back. I am always grateful when a reader chooses my work and I hope you enjoyed it!

With the vast selection available online, I am touched that you chose to be purchasing my work and take valuable time out of your life to read it. My hope is that you feel you made the right decision.

I very much would like to know what you thought of the book. Please take the time to write an honest and informative review on Amazon.com. Your experience and opinions will be of great benefit to me and those readers looking to make an informed choice.

With much thanks,

Valeria Ray

Printed in Great Britain
by Amazon